D1257428

THE CAMERA

By Sandra Pobst

WORLD ALMANAC® LIBRARY

Please visit our web site at: www.worldalmanaclibrary.com
For a free color catalog describing World Almanac® Library's list of high-quality books
and multimedia programs, call 1-800-848-2928 (USA) or 1-800-387-3178 (Canada).
World Almanac® Library's fax: (414) 332-3567.

Library of Congress Cataloging-in-Publication Data

Pobst, Sandy.
    The camera / by Sandy Pobst.
        p. cm. — (Great inventions)
    Includes bibliographical references and index.
    ISBN 0-8368-5801-8 (lib. bdg.)
    1. Photography—History—Juvenile literature. 2. Cameras—
History—Juvenile literature. I. Title.
TR15.P54   2005
770—dc22   2004056931

First published in 2005 by
World Almanac® Library
330 West Olive Street, Suite 100
Milwaukee, WI 53132 USA

A Creative Media Applications, Inc. Production
Design and Production: Alan Barnett, Inc.
Editors: Matt Levine, Susan Madoff
Copy Editor: Laurie Lieb
Proofreader: Laurie Lieb
Indexer: Nara Wood
World Almanac® Library editorial direction: Mark J. Sachner
World Almanac® Library editor: Gini Holland
World Almanac® Library art direction: Tammy West
World Almanac® Library production: Jessica Morris

Photo credits: © AP/Wide World Photos: pages 6, 12, 19, 20, 22, 32, 35, 36, 38, 40; © Archivo
Iconografico, S.A./CORBIS: page 5; © Bettmann/CORBIS: pages 4, 9, 11, 24, 27, 28; © CORBIS:
page 31; © Randy Faris/CORBIS: page 43; © Hulton-Deutsch Collection/CORBIS: page 10, 14;
© Picture History: page 17; © Stapleton Collection/CORBIS: page 30; diagram by Rolin Graphics:
page 23.

Printed in Canada

1 2 3 4 5 6 7 8 9 09 08 07 06 05

TABLE OF CONTENTS

Words that appear in the glossary are printed in
boldface type the first time they appear in the text.

RECORDING OUR WORLD

W hat would the world be like without photography? No snapshots of family and friends. No television. No movies. No photographs to illustrate newspapers, books, and magazines. Imagine taking a vacation, but not having photos to look at afterward. Imagine listening to sporting events, but not seeing the action. Imagine reading about events happening in other countries, but not being able to see the pictures. How would life be different?

Since ancient times, people have wanted to record images of the world around them. Carvings on bones and cave paintings give us some idea of how our earliest

▼ *This drawing of Giovanni Battista della Porta's reflecting light room illustrates how images would travel through a pinhole and reflect back upon the walls of the room.*

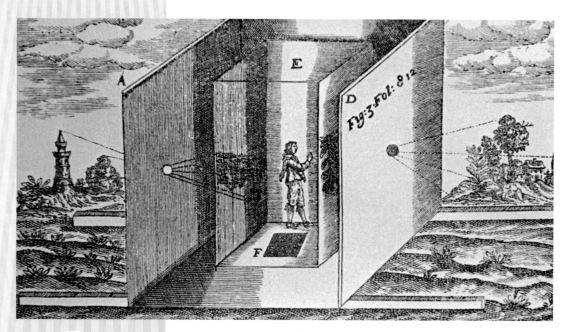

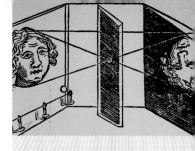

ancestors lived. Over the centuries, artists became more skilled in representing their world. The paintings and drawings that have survived through the years, however, still don't show the world as it was at that moment. Instead, people see the artist's vision of the world.

With the invention of the modern camera in the nineteenth century, life changed dramatically. Before long, photography was not only documenting the world, but influencing and challenging people's opinions and beliefs. Today, photographs, movies, and television shows continue to create, as well as reflect, our culture.

The story of how a simple camera grew to be so powerful began centuries ago. It may have all started when people noticed that magical images sometimes appeared in dark rooms.

Reflecting Light

As early as the fifth century B.C., a Chinese philosopher named Mo-tzu, or Mo Ti (c. 470–c. 391 B.C.), wrote about a "locked treasure room." This darkened room had a small hole in one wall. On sunny days, images from outside the room appeared upside down on the wall opposite the pinhole.

Although this discovery may have seemed like magic, the images appeared in the dark room because of the way light behaves. When people see an object, they are actually looking at the light that reflects off the object. This reflected light travels in a straight line. When it reaches a small opening, the light rays cross each other and create the upside-down image. (This only occurs with small holes. Larger openings scatter the light. The result is a blurry image or just a bright spot.)

Mo-tzu wasn't the only person who noticed what happened when light was focused through a small opening. Aristotle (384–322 B.C.), the Greek philosopher and scholar, also described this principle. Light filtering through the leaves of a shade tree enabled Aristotle to see a partial solar eclipse projected on the ground. By A.D. 1000, Arabian scholars were using small holes made in tents to observe solar activity.

Until the Renaissance, darkened rooms that let in pinhole-sized beams of light were used mainly to study solar events. (The Renaissance was a period in European history—from the fourteenth through the sixteenth centuries—that was marked by developments in the arts and sciences.) As the arts flourished during the Renaissance, artists began using such rooms also. Leonardo da Vinci (1452–1519), the great Italian artist and inventor, was fascinated by the images that could be produced using this principle. He studied the images in such a darkened room to learn more about light and shadow.

▲ *The great artist and inventor Leonardo da Vinci was fascinated by the images he could produce by manipulating light and shadows.*

The darkened room helped artists create more lifelike pictures because the artists could now trace the images that were projected. There were still limits, however. The scenes that could be drawn using this optical tool were limited by the location of the room. The room could be used only on bright, sunny days. The artists still had to carefully trace the scenes that were projected upside-down on the wall. This was a time-consuming process. Although it was a step forward in producing realistic images of daily life, those images were still far from photographs.

The Camera Obscura

Gradually, artists and scientists added features to the darkened rooms to make them easier to use. *Lenses* (shaped pieces of glass) were added to the openings to create sharper, more focused images. Some lenses made the images much larger. Mirrors were also added to the rooms. They allowed the images to be projected onto tables or other surfaces. By the seventeenth century, such a darkened room was known as a **camera obscura**. This name comes from the Latin words for "dark room."

As interest in camera obscuras grew, people experimented with the design. Many were huge, elaborate affairs. One required the artist to enter through a trapdoor in the floor. Others were made using tents so they could be moved from place to place. Over time, however, small wooden boxes became more common as camera obscuras. They were much easier to carry around.

◄ *By the middle of the seventeenth century, the sophisticated darkened room, called a camera obscura, was reduced to the size of a small, portable wooden box.*

Making a Camera Obscura

You can make your own camera obscura with a few everyday items. Just follow these directions.

Materials

▶ Two cardboard tubes (such as those from toilet paper or paper towels)

▶ Tracing paper or wax paper

▶ Black construction paper

▶ Tape

▶ Scissors

▶ Needle or straight pin

Directions

1. Cut the first cardboard tube open lengthwise. Overlap the edges to make it slightly smaller than the second tube. Tape the long edges to hold them in place. This tube should now fit snugly inside the second tube.

2. Cut a piece of tracing paper or wax paper to fit over one end of the smaller tube. Fold the edges of the paper around the tube, and tape them firmly in place.

3. Cut a piece of black construction paper to fit over one end of the larger tube. Fold the edges of the paper around the tube, and tape them firmly in place.

4. Using a needle or straight pin, poke a hole in the center of the black paper.

5. Slide the smaller tube into the larger tube. (The end covered with tracing paper or wax paper should be inserted first.)

6. On a bright day, look through the open end of the smaller tube. An upside-down image should appear on the tracing paper inside the tube. Move the smaller tube in or out to focus the image.

During the seventeenth and eighteenth centuries, artists used their portable camera obscuras to create scenes and portraits with more realistic detail than ever before. With these small camera obscuras, the design of the first modern cameras was established. Photography required a way to automatically record a scene, however, and that was still a century away.

Capturing Light

About the same time as the camera obscura gained popularity, scientists were exploring the properties of various chemicals. They discovered that chemical compounds that contained silver turned dark when they were exposed to the Sun. Most scientists believed that this reaction was due to something in the air or the Sun's heat.

A German scientist, Heinrich Schulze (1687–1744), conducted many experiments with silver compounds. In 1727, he proved that it was light, not heat, that caused the chemicals to turn dark. This turned out to be a key in the development of photography. At the time, however, no one connected silver's chemical reaction to light with the camera obscura craze.

In England, in 1802, Thomas Wedgwood (1771–1805) discovered a way to create an image on paper coated with silver nitrate (a silver compound that turns dark when exposed to light). He placed the paper behind a piece of glass that had a design painted on it. Then he exposed the paper to light. The areas that were dark on the glass appeared light on the paper. Likewise, light areas on the glass showed up dark on the exposed paper. This reversal of dark and light fields was called a **negative image**. This was the first major breakthrough in the field of photography, but there were still many problems to be solved before true photographs could be taken.

The biggest problem was that the image got darker every time it was exposed to the light. Whenever someone viewed the negative image, the paper got a little darker. Before long, the paper would be completely black and the image could no longer be seen. Wedgwood tried to **fix** the image, or stop the development process in order to make the image permanent, but he died before he could find a way to achieve this goal.

▲ *In 1816, Joseph Niepce produced the first permanent negative using his camera obscura with paper coated with silver salts.*

Sun Pictures

Some time after Wedgwood's death, a French inventor named Joseph Niepce (1765–1833) became interested in automatically recording images from a camera obscura. For more than a decade, Niepce patiently experimented with various cameras. He also tried numerous chemicals on different types of recording materials, such as paper, metal, and stone. In 1816, he successfully captured the image of a birdhouse outside his window on a paper coated with silver salts. By washing the paper in an acid, Niepce was able to stop the darkening process and make a permanent image. This solved the problem that Wedgwood had struggled with. However, the image was a negative image. Niepce would not be satisfied until he could find a way to make a positive print.

Next, Niepce decided to try a chemical that turned lighter when exposed to light to produce a **positive image**. In 1822, he began experimenting with a completely different chemical. He tried spreading a type of asphalt called bitumen of Judea on the surface of a metal **plate**. He found that bitumen that was exposed to light hardened and turned a lighter color. Bitumen that had not been exposed to light could be washed off the metal. Niepce called the resulting images *heliographs*, which means "Sun pictures" in Greek.

In the summer of 1826, Niepce placed a metal plate covered with bitumen in a camera obscura. After eight hours, he washed the plate and discovered a faint but clear picture of the view from his window. Niepce had successfully produced the world's first photograph.

The Camera

While Niepce was toiling away on his photographic experiments, Louis-Jacques-Mandé Daguerre (1787–1851), a French artist, was dazzling audiences with a new type of show called a diorama. Daguerre, who began his career painting scenes for the Paris Opera, was fascinated by the effects of light on his paintings. He came up with the idea of painting detailed scenes on fabric-covered screens that stretched 48 by 72 feet (15 by 22 meters). Daguerre used a camera obscura to make the paintings as lifelike as possible. Then he used lights in front of and behind the paintings to highlight particular scenes. As Daguerre moved the lights closer or farther away, he could create a sense of daylight fading or the sun burning through fog. Colored filters on the lights helped create different moods. The elaborate lighting sequences made the figures in his paintings appear to move.

In 1822, Daguerre opened the first diorama theater in Paris, France. Audiences sat in a darkened room similar to today's movie theaters. Daguerre's painted screens were positioned on three sides of the theater. The floor of the theater revolved from screen to screen as the lighting shifted. Music and sound effects, even

▼ Louis-Jacques-Mandé Daguerre's diorama inspired future inventors and led to the development of today's motion pictures.

scents, added dimension to the audience's experience. Viewers watched in awe as people appeared to enter a cathedral to celebrate midnight mass. The audience saw candles being lit in the church and could smell the candles and incense. Another popular diorama showed an avalanche roaring down a Swiss mountainside, covering a small village in snow.

Although the dioramas were very successful, painting the detailed scenes was a lengthy process. Daguerre wanted desperately to find a way to automatically record images on the screens. When he heard the news of Niépce's heliographs, Daguerre contacted the inventor. They began working together in 1829 to develop a process that would produce detailed images. Daguerre financed his share of the photography experiments with his income from the dioramas.

▼ An example of a daguerreotype, invented in 1839. This particular daguerreo-type, a portrait of Abraham Lincoln's wife, Mary Todd Lincoln, illustrates the detail earlier heliographs were unable to achieve.

Success at Last

Niepce and Daguerre worked closely together until Niépce's death in 1833. After that, Daguerre continued the experiments by himself. In January 1839, Daguerre announced that he had succeeded in producing **daguerreotypes**. Daguerre claimed that these clear, detailed images were the world's first photographs, ignoring Niépce's earlier success in producing heliographs. (Because Daguerre's invention gained so much attention, he was long regarded as the inventor of photography. It wasn't until 1952, when Niépce's first photograph was rediscovered, that Niepce was recognized as the world's first successful photographer.)

Daguerre's process included coating a smooth copper plate with silver compounds, then polishing the plate until it gleamed. The plate was then placed in a box filled with iodine fumes. The fumes made the plate more sensitive to light. After a final polishing, the plate was carefully placed inside a camera that had already been focused on the subject. The photographer opened the shutter, exposing the plate to the brightly lit scene for fifteen to twenty minutes. (The camera's *shutter* controls how long the plate or film is exposed to light.)

Mercury vapor was used to develop the image after it had been exposed. The chemical interacted with the silver compound and brightened the light areas of the picture. Daguerre then washed the plate in a salt solution to fix the image (make it permanent).

As word of Daguerre's accomplishment spread, excitement grew. People who saw the first daguerreotypes were astonished at the details that were captured in the images. One French reviewer described the daguerreotype as a "magic mirror," a "faithful memory" of the natural world. Other reports compared daguerreotypes to the finest drawings and predicted that Daguerre's invention would soon replace artists.

A Different Technique

Daguerre was not the only inventor trying to develop a practical photographic process. In England, William Henry Fox Talbot (1800–1877) had been working since 1833 to create a photograph. Instead of metal plates, Talbot used a paper coated with a silver compound. He placed the paper into a camera obscura and exposed the paper to a brightly lit image for twenty seconds to create a negative image that he called a **photogenic drawing**. Like Daguerre, Talbot washed his paper in a salt solution to fix the image.

Photographing Ghosts

The first daguerreotypes captured only those images that stayed still for fifteen to twenty minutes. From the mid-1800s through the early 1900s, some photographers used this knowledge to create photos that appeared to show spirits. When a photograph session was almost over, the "ghost" (a person working with the photographer) would walk to a spot near the person being photographed. After standing in place for a few minutes, the ghost would leave the studio. This brief exposure left a faint, ghost-like image in the background of the photograph.

Most photographers made it clear that such photographs were made to entertain the public. However, William H. Mumler claimed that he had photographed actual ghosts. He was charged with fraud in 1869. Although at least one of the "spirits" in his photographs was proved to be a living person, Mumler's trial ended when the judge dropped the charges for lack of solid evidence.

To create a positive print, Talbot rubbed wax on the paper containing the negative. This made the light areas transparent. The photogenic drawing, or negative, was then placed on top of a new paper coated with the silver compound, exposed once again to light, then washed in a salt solution. This process created a positive image on the second paper, which Talbot called a **calotype**. (The images were also known briefly as Talbotypes.)

In 1839, as soon as he successfully produced a positive image, Talbot notified the French Académie des Sciences and the English Royal Society.

▼ William Henry Fox Talbot's technique of using a negative image to make positive prints is still in use today. In this late nineteenth century picture, Talbot (right) is shown taking a picture of a customer.

Unfortunately for Talbot, Daguerre had announced his daguerreotype a few weeks earlier. Despite the fact that Daguerre is often credited with the invention of photography, Talbot's technique had a far greater impact on the development of photography than Daguerre's did. Talbot's basic process of using a negative image to make an unlimited number of positive prints is still used in film photography today.

Competition

Following the announcements of the daguerreotype and the calotype, interest in photography skyrocketed. People debated the advantages of the two inventions. Daguerre's process resulted in beautifully detailed images with silver tones, making it the favorite choice

The Camera

for portrait photography. Although calotype images were slightly blurred, people could make multiple photographs from the paper negative. The paper used to produce calotypes was also much cheaper than the copper plates used for daguerreotypes.

Daguerreotypes were not easy to produce. They required a great deal of equipment and skill. The plates, camera, and boxes used for developing daguerreotypes were bulky and hard to move around. As a result, photographers specializing in daguerreotypes usually offered their services in a studio setting. Anyone posing for a daguerreotype had to sit or stand very still for a long period of time, or the final image would be blurred. The earliest daguerreotypes required exposures of up to twenty minutes. By the 1850s, exposure time had been reduced to a minute or less, but it was still difficult to remain completely still for that long. To help the person keep the pose, photographers often used special chairs with metal braces that held the person's head firmly in place. The biggest disadvantage of daguerreotypes was the inability to make copies. If a daguerreotype was scratched, which happened frequently, the image was ruined and could not be replaced.

A New Industry

The daguerreotype was announced in January 1839. In August of that same year, the French government bought the **patent** to Daguerre's process. Declaring that photography was France's gift to the world, the government provided information about the daguerreotype process at no charge.

This openness fueled the public's interest in photography. Daguerre demonstrated his process in lectures and provided directions for building daguerreotype

Samuel F. B. Morse (1791–1872)

Samuel F. B. Morse, the American inventor of the telegraph, was an artist as well as an inventor. Morse, a good friend of Louis Daguerre, learned to take daguerreotypes in France soon after the process was invented. Then he brought the technique back to the United States and established one of the first daguerreotype studios in America. One of his students, Mathew Brady (1823?–1896), later became one of America's most famous photographers.

Cameras—Then and Now

Although cameras have improved tremendously since Niepce's time, the basic structure remains the same. At its simplest, a camera is a light-proof box with a shutter that admits light and a lens that focuses the image. The images are recorded on a light-sensitive material, such as specially treated plates, paper, or film. In digital cameras, the images are recorded on computer chips.

In the early days of photography, shutters were operated by hand because the chemicals coating the plates were not extremely sensitive to light. The shutter had to be open up to twenty minutes to produce a detailed photograph. Over time, inventors discovered more light-sensitive materials, and cameras were fitted with mechanical shutters that allowed light in for just a fraction of a second. Today, a computer chip in a camera often controls both the shutter and the lens. The chip determines how long the shutter needs to be open. It also focuses the image automatically.

Fast Fact

Photographs could not be printed in newspapers and magazines until 1881, when the halftone process was invented. The halftone process breaks photographic images into a series of dots that can be reproduced in print.

cameras. Soon, books about photography were being published. Camera makers set up shop, offering their services to people who didn't want to build their own camera. Stores offered photographic chemicals and other supplies. Daguerreotype studios became common sights in major cities throughout Europe and the United States. Galleries began offering calotypes and daguerreotypes for sale. A brand-new industry had been launched.

The growing popularity of photographs was also beginning to change society. For the first time, middle-class families could afford to have their portraits made. These lifelike images provided treasured mementos of family members to pass down to future generations. Photographs were also used to fight crime, as police forces began to put photographs of wanted criminals on posters.

3 RAPID CHANGES

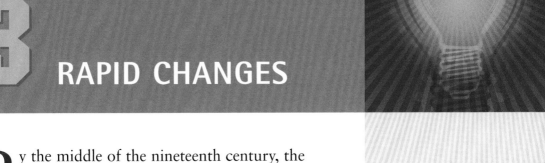

By the middle of the nineteenth century, the photographic portrait industry was booming. Inventors continued to try to find a technique that combined the advantages of both the daguerreotype and the calotype.

A Revolutionary Idea

In 1851, Frederick Scott Archer (1813–1857) accomplished this goal. Using glass plates instead of metal or paper, Archer developed a process that produced clear, detailed negatives that could be used to print multiple copies of a photograph.

Archer first coated the glass plate with **collodion** (a sticky liquid mixture) and then soaked it in a chemical bath. This created a layer of silver bromide,

▼ In 1853, an advertisement in a photographic journal showed this picture of the interior view of the Meade Brothers' Daguerreotype Gallery in New York City. Customers could come to the gallery to have their picture taken or purchase daguerrotypes.

A Flash in Time

Before the invention of the light bulb (in 1879), most photographers relied upon natural lighting for their photographs. In the 1860s, however, some photographers began burning magnesium wires when they needed more light. By the 1880s, magnesium flashlamps were widely used. Soon, photographers were mixing other flammable chemicals with the magnesium to create flash powders. These were easily lit with candles or sparks. Unfortunately, the chemicals often exploded, and many photographers lost their hands or arms in accidents.

a chemical that is very sensitive to light. The glass plate was placed in a camera while it was still wet, exposed to light for a few seconds, and then placed in a solution to develop the negative image. Archer's invention became known as **wet-plate photography**.

There were many advantages to the new wet-plate process. Glass plates were considerably cheaper than the copper plates used for daguerreotypes, and the prints were much clearer than those made from calotypes.

As exciting as this new technique was, it still had some practical obstacles that photographers had to work around. The glass plates had to be coated with collodion and loaded into the camera in a darkened space. Once the picture was taken, the plates had to be developed immediately. If a plate dried out at any point, the image was ruined.

Cheap Imitations

The new wet-plate process led to two other inventions that made photographs available to anybody who wanted them. The creator of the collodion process, Frederick Archer, worked with Peter Fry to develop **ambrotypes**. These photographs were actually wet-plate negatives placed over a black background. They resembled daguerreotypes but were much cheaper.

Tintypes were a variation on ambrotypes. Instead of glass plates, photographers used thin metal plates that had been painted black and coated with collodion. After the tintype was developed, a positive image appeared on the plate. Tintypes were cheap, costing only a few cents. They became very popular during the Civil War (1861–1865), as soldiers and their families exchanged photographs in letters.

Documenting History

With the need for long exposures removed, photographers suddenly had more choice in what they could photograph. Many traveled to foreign countries to photograph people from other cultures, natural wonders, historic landmarks, and soldiers on the battlefield.

▼ *Mathew Brady's images of the deaths and destruction caused by the Civil War documented one of the most tragic episodes in American history. His contributions to photojournalism helped legitimate the field as a bona fide addition to news reporting.*

Mathew Brady was one photographer who was well aware of the power of photographs. In 1860, Abraham Lincoln was running for president. During the campaign, a portrait that Brady had taken of Lincoln appeared on the cover of *Harper's Weekly,* a widely read newspaper of that era. For the first time, voters throughout the country could see an image of

Mathew Brady (1823?–1896)

Mathew Brady believed firmly in the ability of photography to record and influence history. At the age of sixteen, Brady studied photography with Samuel Morse. Within five years, Brady had earned a reputation as one of the best portrait photographers in America.

In 1856, Brady moved to Washington, D.C. Claiming that "the camera is the eye of history," he sought to make portraits of influential Americans. Today, Brady is recognized as the first documentary photographer. His collection of Civil War photographs is on display in the National Portrait Gallery of the Smithsonian Institution in Washington, D.C., and online at the Library of Congress Web site.

the man who was running for president while reading about his political views. The picture gave Lincoln a definite advantage, because his main opponent, Stephen Douglas, did not receive the same publicity. After winning the election, Lincoln said, "Make no mistake, gentlemen. Brady made me president."

Brady's most ambitious effort was documenting the Civil War through photographs. He hired twenty photographers who were skilled in the wet-plate process and gave them wagons to use as darkrooms. These men traveled from battlefield to battlefield, photographing the bloody conflict. Their unforgettable photographs, published under Brady's name, were the first to record actual images of war.

Simplifying the Process

The next big advance in photography was an invention by Richard Leach Maddox (1816–1902), an English doctor. In 1871, chemicals in collodion began causing health problems for the doctor. Maddox wrote an article suggesting that gelatin (a substance obtained from the hooves and bones of animals) could be used in place of the collodion.

This new process proved to be even more successful than Maddox had hoped. Not only could the new **emulsion** be allowed to dry on the plates, it was much more sensitive to light than the collodion. In addition, after the photographs were taken, there was no rush to develop the glass-plate negatives. They could be stored in a dark place until the photographer was ready to make prints.

The **dry-plate photography** process required less than a second's exposure to record an image, so action shots could be captured for the first time. These pictures that took only an instant to capture became known as snapshots.

New Cameras

The advantages of the dry-plate process required new camera designs. New cameras had a mechanical device that controlled the shutter. The springs or rubber bands that connected the mechanism with the shutter enabled photographers to expose the dry plates for just a fraction of a second. New cameras also had viewfinders, special lenses on the outside of the camera box that allowed users to see what they were photographing.

Cameras began featuring distance scales. These markings helped a photographer adjust the camera lens for the best results, depending on the distance between the camera and the subject in the photo.

These design changes improved the quality of photographs. They also allowed camera makers to produce smaller, more portable cameras. Cameras designed for amateurs used plates that were 5 by 8 inches (12.7 by 20.3 centimeters) or smaller.

While the innovations in camera design made it easier to take photographs, the process was still too complicated and expensive for most people. In the years to come, this too would change.

Settling a Bet

In the early 1870s, California governor and racehorse owner Leland Stanford bet his friends that galloping horses lifted all four feet off the ground at the same time. No one knew for certain how horses' legs moved when they ran, because the motion was too fast for the human eye to follow.

To prove his point, Stanford hired landscape photographer Eadweard Muybridge (1830–1904) to photograph his horse in motion. Although the cameras were now fast enough to capture the horse's movement, only one photo could be taken at a time.

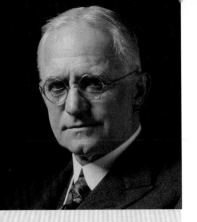

George Eastman (1854–1932)

George Eastman was born in Waterville, New York. He established the Eastman Dry Plate Company. This business would make dramatic changes in American society.

In his later years, Eastman donated most of his fortune to charities and universities. In 1930, he was diagnosed with spinal stenosis, a disease that affected his spinal cord. It became increasingly difficult and painful for Eastman to move about. Faced with the prospect of having to depend upon others for his care, Eastman settled his affairs. Then, on March 14, 1932, he shot himself and ended his life. The note he left said simply, "My work is done—why wait?"

Muybridge came up with the idea of setting up twenty-four cameras along a track. Each camera shutter was connected to a thin wire that stretched across the horse's path. As the horse ran past each camera, it tripped the wires and operated the shutters.

When the plates were developed, they showed that all four feet do indeed leave the ground while a horse is running. Muybridge had successfully photographed a horse in motion, and Stanford won his bet.

In the mid-1880s, Muybridge began photographing other animals in motion, including humans. Three years later, in 1887, he published more than 20,000 images in a book called *Animal Locomotion*. This comprehensive book is still used as a resource by many artists and scientists.

The Eastman Dry Plate Company

In the 1870s, in Rochester, New York, George Eastman (1854–1932) began experimenting with different formulas, or recipes, for a dry plate emulsion. By 1879, Eastman was convinced he had a winning formula. He also had a design for a machine that could automate the process of coating the glass plates with emulsion. After patenting his inventions, Eastman opened a factory to mass-produce the plates. In 1880, he founded the Eastman Dry Plate Company in Rochester.

Making It Simple

In 1884, after much experimentation, Eastman found a way to make flexible, paper-backed film that could be wound into rolls. The rolls would allow photographers to take up to twenty-four pictures before having to change the film. Eastman worked with a camera maker named William H. Walker to design

The Camera

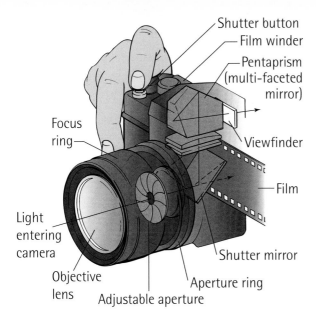

Shutter button
Film winder
Pentaprism (multi-faceted mirror)
Viewfinder
Focus ring
Film
Light entering camera
Shutter mirror
Objective lens
Aperture ring
Adjustable aperture

a roll holder that would fit onto existing cameras. The next year, Eastman's company began selling the new, flexible roll film and roll holders.

In 1888, the Eastman Company began selling the Kodak camera. It was so small that it could be held in one hand. Inside was enough film for one hundred photographs. When customers finished taking all the pictures, they simply mailed their cameras to the Eastman Company. There, employees removed the film, processed the negatives, and printed the photos. The cameras were loaded with another roll of film and mailed back to the customer, along with the photographs. The advertisements for the Kodak camera summed it up neatly: "You press the button, and we do the rest."

Within a year, Eastman had sold thirteen thousand Kodak cameras. As many as seventy rolls of film were being developed each day.

In 1900, the Eastman Kodak Company announced its latest camera, the Brownie. Designed for children, the Brownie cost one dollar. It was an overnight success. Within a year, over 250,000 people owned a Brownie. Eastman's dream of making photography available to everyone had come true.

4 MOVING PICTURES

▼ *The entertainment provided by the magic lantern, shown below, inspired many inventors to improve upon the idea of a still image, leading to the invention and evolution of moving pictures.*

Throughout history, people have been fascinated by pictures that seem to move. Over time, artists learned to use several different kinds of special effects to show movement in pictures. Each improvement took the world one step closer to real motion pictures, or movies.

Early Illusions

As early as the seventeenth century, the **magic lantern** —a wooden box with a lens on one side and a candle or lamp inside — was a popular form of entertainment. Glass slides holding images from popular stories were placed into the magic lantern between the lens and the light. The lantern projected the pictures onto a wall or screen. A good lantern operator could change slides very quickly, making it seem as though the characters in the pictures were moving. Similarly, as we have seen, in the early 1800s, Louis Daguerre's dioramas made a stir by making audiences believe they were watching people move about on screen. Daguerre accomplished this by controlling the lighting, music, sound effects, and even the scents in the air. All of these effects combined to make audiences feel as though they were seeing pictures move.

Transforming Toys into Movies

In 1834, a new toy was introduced in Britain. Called the Zoetrope ("wheel of life"), the toy looked like an open-ended drum on a stand. A series of pictures was painted on the inside of the drum. Slits ran from the top edge of the drum to the middle. The drum was spun around on the stand. A person looking through the slits saw the pictures magically appear to move.

The Zoetrope worked because of something called *persistence of vision*. When the human eye sees something, that image remains on the retina at the back of the eye for a brief moment after the object moves from view. When a series of still images moves quickly past the eye, the lingering images blur together slightly, giving the impression of moving pictures.

In 1876, an inventor in France named Emile Reynaud (1844–1918) placed a smaller, mirrored cylinder in the center of a drum similar to that used in the Zoetrope. The animated pictures were drawn on bands of paper that fit inside the drum. As the drum spun around, the pictures on the paper strip were reflected in the mirrored cylinder. By 1888, Reynaud had patented the Projecting Praxinoscope, which enabled him to show moving pictures on a large screen. This represented a giant step toward modern motion pictures.

The Kinetograph and Kinetoscope

In 1889, Thomas Edison (1847–1931) saw the flexible, transparent film that the Eastman Kodak Company had invented. Edison, America's leading inventor, who later invented the lightbulb, had recently invented the phonograph, a machine that recorded and played back sound. Edison believed that if he could make a machine to record and

The Photo Gun

A French scientist named Étienne-Jules Marey (1830–1904) wanted to use photography to study the flight of birds. After studying a "photographic revolver" invented by French astronomer Pierre-Jules Janssen (1824–1907), Marey changed the invention to suit his purposes.

In 1882, Marey altered a rifle so that it could be used to take pictures. He removed the bullet chamber and attached a special camera that held disk-shaped glass plates. The camera used a trigger action similar to that found on a machine gun. Whenever the trigger was pulled, the shutter opened and closed over and over automatically until the trigger was released. Pulling the trigger also moved the glass photo disk to a new position. Marey's first photo gun allowed the user to take twelve photographs per second. By the time Marey had finished tinkering with his invention, he could take as many as 120 pictures per second.

play back moving pictures, it could be used with his phonograph.

Edison chose one of his assistants, William Laurie Kennedy Dickson (1860–1935), to work on the design for a motion picture camera and projector. By late 1889, Dickson had produced the Kinetograph, the world's first movie camera. Small holes in the film strip fit over sprockets (teeth) on the gears of the Kinetograph and kept the film from slipping while the pictures were being taken. A special mechanism moved the film behind the shutter and stopped it while each picture was taken. Electricity was used to power the camera.

One of Edison and Dickson's first movies was of a man sneezing. The Kinetograph was an amazing machine, but it was not very practical. It weighed more than 1 ton (0.9 metric tons) and took up more space than a piano.

With the movie camera built, Dickson was ready to start on the projector, which would be called the

The Camera

Kinetoscope. The first Kinetoscope opened in 1894 in New York City and became an instant hit. Viewers took turns putting a penny in the machine and cranking a handle to view the thirty-second movies known as "peep shows."

The Lumière Brothers

After studying the the Kinetograph machine, two French brothers, Auguste (1862–1954) and Louis Lumière (1864–1948), came up with an improved combination camera and projector in 1895. The new invention was called the Cinématographe. It had a mechanical claw that hooked into the holes along the side of the film and pulled it forward. It became known as a stop-motion device and is still used in movie cameras today.

The Cinématographe weighed only 16 pounds (7.2 kg) and could easily be carried to any location. It was powered by a hand crank rather than electricity, so it could be used any-where. Unlike the Kinetoscope, which projected small images within a box-sized space, the Lumière brothers' machine projected life-size images on a screen.

The brothers rented theater space and began advertising their first show. Only thirty-five people attended on opening night, but within weeks the Lumières were showing their films to more than two thousand people a day.

The films featured events from daily life, such as a baby playing and factory workers taking a break. In one film, a train pulling into the station appeared to be coming right at the audience. Viewers screamed in fright and ran from the room. Audiences, fascinated with the life-size spectacles, watched the movies over and over again.

▲ *Auguste and Louis Lumière showed the first moving pictures in 1895, in a darkened theater, just as we watch movies today.*

A New Approach

As the nineteenth century drew to an end, people became bored with films that showed everyday events. A French magician named Georges Méliès (1861–1938) was determined to bring his own kind of magic to the screen. After accidentally discovering how to make one scene fade into another, Méliès became known as the master of special effects. He built elaborate sets and hired actors to perform stories as he filmed them.

By 1903, a former motion picture operator in the United States named Edwin S. Porter (1870–1941) was editing films to make them more exciting. He used several different techniques, including cutting back and forth between different scenes and showing events from different points of view. His famous 1903 film, *The Great Train Robbery,* featured the first chase scene ever shown in the movies.

When America's first movie theater opened in Pittsburgh, Pennsylvania, in 1905, people flocked to see Porter's movies. Admission was a nickel, so people began calling the movie theater a *nickelodeon*. Before long, the nickelodeon was averaging 20,000 customers a week.

▲ *Georges Méliès brought special effects to motion pictures. This picture, showing a frame from his 1902* A Trip to the Moon, *illustrates the kind of storytelling he was able to do with elaborate sets and a keen imagination.*

The Talkies

In 1916, the Western Electric Company successfully linked movies and sound with the invention of the Vitaphone, but movie studios still did not jump at the chance to make talking pictures. They were already making billions of dollars with silent movies. Setting

Regulating Morality

By the end of the 1920s, some people worried that children and young adults who watched movies that featured drug use or immoral behavior might imitate that type of behavior. In response, the Motion Picture Producers and Distributors of America (MPPDA) created a code of ethics in 1930. Known informally as the Hays Code, it spelled out exactly what could and couldn't be shown in the movies.

Studios largely ignored the code until 1934, when Congress threatened to make laws forcing the studios to follow the code. From that point until a new ratings code was put into effect in 1968, the Hays Code limited the content of American movies.

up studios and theaters to include sound systems would cost a lot of money and decrease their profits.

In 1920, however, the radio was invented. Entertainment audiences would soon grow to appreciate sound and expect it. Within five years, fifty million families owned radios. Most people chose to stay home and listen to the lively shows produced on radio instead of going to a silent movie theater.

Faced with bankruptcy, a movie company called Warner Brothers decided to gamble on adding sound to its films. It bought the Vitaphone from Western Electric and outfitted a theater with sound equipment. In 1926, the movie *Don Juan* became the first motion picture to incorporate sound. Although the soundtrack consisted of music only, the movie was an instant success. Warner Brothers followed up with *The Jazz Singer* in 1927, starring Al Jolson, a popular singer and actor. This time, Jolson talked and sang during the film. Audiences were dazzled. They soon demanded more talking pictures. Even during the Great Depression of the 1930s, when many families could barely scrape together enough money to pay for necessities, attendance at the movies grew.

Fast Fact

Movie stars influenced many aspects of American life—especially fashion. Women began wearing pillbox hats and trench coats, imitating actress Greta Garbo. Sales of men's undershirts plummeted in 1934 after heartthrob Clark Gable appeared in *It Happened One Night* without an undershirt under his dress shirt.

CHAPTER 5

CHANGING FOCUS

In the early twentieth century, as movies began to have a greater impact on American values and customs than photography, the documentary role of photography continued, reporting newsworthy events and recording everyday life. Photographers often used their images to lobby for social change. Photography also finally began receiving recognition and acceptance as an art form.

▶ *This portrait by Julia Margaret Cameron was taken in the late nineteenth century. Believing that there was artistry in capturing reality, Cameron purposely softened the focus on her subjects to create a more beautiful image.*

Art or Science?

In the early days of photography, much emphasis was placed upon the equipment needed to take a picture. Many people believed that because the camera was recording the image, photography was more a science than an art.

Some photographers disagreed. Julia Margaret Cameron (1815–1879), for example, purposely softened the focus of the portraits she took. This gave the images a dreamy, romantic look that became Cameron's trademark. Other photographers argued that such techniques were not necessary in order to consider photographs as art. They claimed that the skillful arrangement of elements in the photograph was what made it art. In this view, a sharply focused photograph was ideal.

Throughout the nineteenth century, the public tended to regard photographs as historical records, proof that events had really happened. As new cameras and processes were introduced, photographers had more flexibility in their subjects. The power of photographs to influence social policies gradually became apparent. One of the best examples of this power was Congress's decision to make Yellowstone a national park after seeing photographs of its beauty.

As the twentieth century began, photojournalism and documentary photography gained importance. Photographers such as Jacob Riis (1849–1914) and Lewis Hine (1874–1940) used their strong images to shape public policy. Riis's photographs of immigrant life in New York City slums convinced city leaders to strengthen laws improving living conditions for thousands. Hines documented the widespread use of child labor. He believed that once people saw the horrid conditions in his photographs, they would demand laws to end child labor. Later, photographers

Alfred Stieglitz (1864–1946)

In the early 1900s after traveling and working in Europe, Alfred Stieglitz settled in New York City, where the energetic, urban atmosphere inspired him. Using the city and its inhabitants as his subject, he would often wait in the street for hours until a moment of observation inspired him. Stieglitz relied on natural elements like snow or fog to create mood in his photographs. His realistic pictures often had double meaning. He would photograph dirty, polluted train yards full of powerful and majestic machines to bring understanding to the viewer that great progress can sometimes have unintended effects. In 1902, Stieglitz founded the quarterly magazine *Camera Work*, which featured the work of new photographers and elevated the medium to a widely accepted art form.

such as Dorothea Lange (1895–1965) were hired by the Farm Security Administration to document changes in American life during the Great Depression.

Only in the early twentieth century did photography finally gain widespread acceptance as art. This recognition was due in large part to the efforts of a group of avant-garde photographers known as the Photo-Secession. Led by Alfred Stieglitz (1864–1946), the Photo-Secession declared that it didn't matter how art was made. What mattered was the end result. Stieglitz published a magazine called *Camera Work,* which brought attention to some of the best and most original photographers in the world, including Edward Steichen (1879–1973) and Gertrude Kasebier (1852–1934).

Another important photographic society, Group f/64, was established on the West Coast in the 1920s. Members concentrated on still lifes, landscapes, and portraits. The most famous photographer in Group f/64 was Ansel Adams (1902–1984). Adams's photographs of the beauty of Yosemite National Park in northern California, which he often enhanced in his dark room, remain some of the most moving images of the natural world.

After World War II (1939–1945), photography came into its own as an art form. Art schools included courses on photography. Photography exhibits grew more common at museums. Since the 1960s, mixed media compositions that combine photography, printmaking, and computer-generated art have become popular.

New Technology

In 1925, the Ernst Leitz Company in Germany announced the Leica camera. The Leica was the first still camera to use 35-millimeter (35mm) film, the same film that was used by the motion picture industry. The 35mm film was very fast (sensitive to light), so photographers rarely needed flashes. Professional photographers soon adopted small, easy-to-use 35mm cameras.

Another technological breakthrough came in 1936. The KineExacta camera, the first single-lens reflex (SLR) camera, was invented in Germany. An SLR camera uses a slanted mirror and a prism to reflect the exact image that will be recorded on film through the camera's viewfinder.

Professional photographers embraced the new SLR cameras. Telephoto and wide-angle lenses allowed photographers to capture views from very far away, as well as close-up shots. Flash guns provided lighting for indoor photos. These features, along with the development of fast film, made the SLR camera a popular choice for both professional and amateur photographers.

Today, SLR cameras still offer photographers great control over their final prints. The best SLR cameras have both automatic and manual adjustment options. As digital technology improves, digital SLR cameras have gained popularity among professional photographers.

Color Photography

Recording color images on film and accurately printing color photographs is a tricky business. Although the first color film was invented in 1930, it was slow to be accepted. Developing the negatives was a complicated process, and few people could manage it at home. It wasn't until Eastman Kodak came out with Kodacolor film in 1949 that color photography was widely accepted. By the 1960s, most people were taking color photographs rather than black-and-white.

Photography during the World Wars

The first half of the twentieth century brought many changes to the world. Although the United States didn't get involved in World War I (1914–1918) until 1917, American reporters traveled to Europe to photograph the conflict.

World War I was the first time that photography was used as a tool in wartime. Aerial photography (taking pictures from the air) was used for the first time to find enemy operations. The Eastman Kodak Company invented an aerial mapping camera that could hold 50 feet (15.2 m) of film. George Eastman volunteered his employees to train members of the U.S. Air Force in the use of the camera. At the end of the war, Eastman refunded all the money the government had paid his company for the training, stating that he did not wish to make a profit from the war or his service to his country.

As the 1930s drew to a close, tensions in Europe were rising. Germany, which had been defeated in World War I, was aggressively pushing to regain its lost power. The Nazi dictator, Adolf Hitler, used movies to build national unity and support his racist viewpoint. These movies were early examples of propaganda films (films that are made to influence people's beliefs).

In 1939, Germany invaded Poland, triggering World War II (1939–1945). Once again, photography was an important tool in the war effort. Aerial photography had grown more sophisticated in pin-pointing enemy locations and supplies. Engineers also photographed the metal parts used to build ships and planes to make sure there were no flaws.

Instant Photos

In the early 1940s, Edwin H. Land (1909–1991) was photographing his three-year-old daughter. She wanted to see the pictures right then and asked why she had to wait. The question triggered an idea in Land's mind. Why couldn't photographs be developed instantly and automatically? He set out to find the answer.

As a student at Harvard University in Massachusetts, Land had worked on a filter that would *polarize*, or control the vibrations of, light waves. His polarizing filter did a fine job of controlling glare from streetlights and neon signs, but most companies felt it would be too expensive to add to their products.

Land started tinkering with polarizing filters and crystals. By 1947, he had invented the Polaroid Land camera. It could take a snapshot and develop a positive print in minutes.

The first Polaroid photographs required the user to fix the image by rubbing a stick coated with chemicals over the surface of the photograph after it emerged from the camera. Later, Land developed a mechanism inside the camera that pushed the film between two rollers. The pressure activated development chemicals that automatically spread over the film when the photograph was pulled from the camera.

▲ Edwin Land (left) changed the way people took pictures with his invention of the Polaroid Land camera in 1947. Suddenly, taking pictures provided instant pleasure and fun to the photographer and subject.

6 IMPROVING THE VIEW

The last half of the twentieth century was a period of rapid development in many different fields. Advances made in electronics, for instance, made cameras easier to use. Improved electronics also led to the development of a brand-new technology: digital photography.

Automatic Adjustments

Today's film cameras have many automatic features, thanks to ever-shrinking computer chips. These electronic components adjust the focus based on the type of shot, such as portrait or landscape. They can also determine the exposure time based on the amount of light available. If the light is too low, an automatic flash is triggered. These cameras are often called "point-and-shoot" cameras, since the user doesn't need to know anything about cameras in order to take a photograph. Some cameras allow more experienced photographers the option of turning off all the automatic features in order to make the adjustments manually.

In the early 1990s, an international group of camera and

▼ An early camera featuring the Advanced Photo System (APS), developed in 1995. APS results in better prints thanks to computerized communication between the camera, film, and photofinishing equipment.

film manufacturers began developing the Advanced Photo System (APS). They announced the new system in 1995. The key to the system is a magnetic coating on the APS film that allows the camera, film, and photofinishing equipment to communicate. When a picture is taken, the exposure and size of the photo are recorded on the magnetic coating. When the film cartridge is developed, the photofinishing equipment automatically reads the magnetic coating and uses that information to produce the best print.

Digital Cameras

A new type of camera was introduced in 1990, following rapid advances in computer technology. Digital cameras do not use film. Instead, tiny computer chips in the cameras analyze light patterns and record images as a series of 0s and 1s. Computers and photo printers then translate the numbers back into images.

Having images in a digital format gives photographers a great deal of flexibility. The images can be printed as photographs or sent to other people over the Internet, either as e-mail attachments or postings on Web sites. Special computer software packages

Great Ideas Never Die

George Eastman transformed photography when he introduced the first Kodak camera. What could be simpler than buying a camera that was already loaded with film, then returning the entire camera to have the film developed?

Sound familiar? It should. In the 1980s, a century after Eastman introduced his great idea, preloaded cameras were being sold to consumers once again. This time, advances in plastics technology allowed manufacturers to produce cheap plastic camera bodies that could be thrown away after one use. Since the 1990s, these bodies have been made from plastic that can be recycled.

▲ *The digital camera, the latest innovation in photographic technology, was developed in the early 1990s. It uses computer technology to produce images that can be improved and edited in a variety of ways.*

allow users to easily edit, or change, the images. Editing a photo may be as simple as resizing the image. It can also involve major changes to the colors and composition, resulting in a completely new image.

Digital cameras have exploded in popularity in recent years. While they are still more expensive than film-based cameras, their prices have become much more affordable. Camera makers predict that soon half of all cameras sold will be digital cameras.

Digital cameras aren't limited to still photography. Digital movie cameras are also available. Like digital photographs, digital movies can be viewed on a computer and sent over the Internet. The movies can be copied to a computer disk, CD-ROM, or DVD for safe storage. Because the best digital movie cameras can record high-quality movies at a fraction of the cost of traditional movie cameras, they have allowed many independent filmmakers to create films without the backing of a studio.

Science and Photography

While photography gained acceptance as a form of art in the twentieth century, its role in science also expanded. The development of special lenses and ultra-fast film has made it possible to photograph everything from the smallest organisms to the farthest planets.

Today, scientists in nearly every field use photographs to document their research or to capture images for further study. Scientists studying extremely small objects use both digital and 35mm film cameras to record images seen under powerful microscopes. Some of the microscopes magnify objects to half a million times their actual size.

Astronomers use special digital cameras attached to telescopes to photograph stars, planets, and other

The Camera

objects in space. The Hubble Space Telescope was fitted with special digital cameras and launched into space in 1990. As it orbits 375 miles (600 kilometers) above Earth, the Hubble's cameras record images and transmit them electronically to scientists around the world.

Oceanographic cameras are housed in steel casings to protect them from underwater pressure. Oceanographers use the cameras to gather data about the depth and surface of the ocean floor.

Biologists sometimes modify cameras and fit them to animals to record their actions in their native habitats. In 2002, scientists attached special cameras to Weddell seals in the Antarctic. The cameras not only recorded information about how the seals navigate and hunt for fish, but also gathered new information about Antarctic fish.

Geologists study pictures taken from satellites orbiting Earth to learn more about Earth's surface. The information in the photographs, for example, can help scientists predict where earthquakes will occur.

Photographing the Stars

The development of digital cameras and computerized telescopes brought the stars within reach of amateur photographers, as well as scientists. One such astrophotographer, Russell Croman of Texas, has gained recognition in both scientific and artistic circles for the photographs he has taken of the Great Orion Nebula and other scenes from space.

To take the pictures, Croman uses one of several telescopes he owns and a special digital camera. Many of the photos require a long exposure, sometimes over more than one night. Once the images are recorded on his computer, Croman processes them to enhance the display. For example, he assigns colors to each type of gas, such as red for sulfur, green for hydrogen, and blue for oxygen. The results are breathtaking views of space that most people would never otherwise see.

IMAGINING THE FUTURE

Changing History

Photographic images still have the power to influence public opinion and change lives.

In 1963, the Southern Christian Leadership Conference (SCLC) organized a civil rights march in Birmingham, Alabama. Thousands of school-age children and youths marched in the streets to protest segregation. Police commissioner Eugene "Bull" Connor ordered violent tactics to break up the crowds. Within hours, images of the brutal actions were blazoned across television screens and the front pages of newspapers around the world. The public was outraged. A year later, in June 1964, the Civil Rights Act became law. The photos from Birmingham and other civil rights marches hastened this process by motivating millions of Americans to demand equal rights for all citizens, regardless of color.

In the mid-1960s and early 1970s, as American involvement in the Vietnam War (1959–1975) grew more intense, photographs from the war zone documented the violent horrors that soldiers faced

▼ Photographs of news events around the country, like this civil rights march, have influenced people to make changes in the way the United States is governed.

daily. Many images from that conflict are seared into the American public's memory of the war: a Saigon police chief executing his prisoner in the streets of the city; a twelve-year-old girl, badly burned when her village was bombed; solemn, flag-draped coffins of American soldiers killed in action.

As more and more photographs were published, public opinion regarding America's participation in Vietnam shifted. Polls reported that a majority of Americans opposed their country's continuing involvement in the Vietnam War.

The list of photographs that have influenced and changed history continues to grow. In 1989, the picture of a lone Chinese protester facing a line of government tanks in Tiananmen Square led to international pressure on the Chinese government to address human rights violations. Broadcasts of a video showing the beating of a man named Rodney King by police in 1991 forced the Los Angeles, California, police department to improve training and supervision of officers. These images, along with many others, demonstrate the role that photographers play in shaping world history.

Ethics in the Digital Age

Nearly all professional photographers today use digital cameras. The move to a digital format raises many ethical questions. (*Ethics* are the set of values by which a person judges what is right or wrong.) One of the most important questions facing photographers is whether or how much to alter, or change, a photograph.

Minor changes may involve the removal of distracting elements (such as power lines) from the background or correcting the color of the photograph. More extreme changes include combining parts of two or more photos or removing people from a photograph. These changes are usually made in an effort to make a photograph more compelling or to improve the composition.

In one recent example, a photographer for the Associated Press (AP) submitted a photo showing people in a Chinese province trying to cross flooded streets. The AP later learned that the photographer had digitally altered the photograph to make it more dramatic. The changes made the floodwaters seem much higher than they actually were. (The AP notified newspapers that the photo shouldn't be published.)

Most people agree that news photos should never be altered. Such photos are powerful because they capture real moments in history. In digital photography, however, changes can be made that no one can detect.

The problem of presenting a photograph as real when it has been altered is not limited to professionals in the print media. The Internet has helped many amateurs distribute photographs that have been changed. One example from 2001 showed a man holding a cat that supposedly weighed 87 pounds (39.5 kg) and measured more than 5 feet (1.5 m) from nose to tail. While many of the photos that make their way around the world are meant for amusement, some people seek to influence public opinion by presenting false images.

During the 2004 presidential campaign, a picture was sent around the Internet that supposedly showed presidential candidate John Kerry speaking at a rally with an antiwar activist. The picture was intended to discredit Kerry. In fact, the image had been created from two separate photos taken a year apart. In the past, people believed that the camera never lied. Today, however, people are learning to question the accuracy of all photographic images.

Big Brother Is Watching

Another dilemma facing Americans in the digital age is whether the right to privacy is more important than security measures. After the terrorist bombings of September 11, 2001, video surveillance cameras were installed in and around government buildings that were considered to be possible terrorist targets. Special face-recognition software installed with the cameras promises the ability to identify individuals. Critics of the systems note that this type of software could eventually be used to track the movements of any person appearing in a public space. They argue that its effectiveness is not in preventing crime, but rather in gathering private information about American citizens. Future generations will have to determine whether the government and private businesses have a right to track an individual's actions and movements with cameras.

Looking Back

From the beginning, people recognized the power of photography. The photographs of the past two centuries have recorded much more than historical events. They also reflect the cultural and social realities of a particular era.

Looking back at all of the innovations that have been made in the field of photography, it is amazing to realize that many of the most important breakthroughs were made by ordinary people whose hobby was taking pictures. As they searched for easier or better ways to do things, they discovered solutions that made—and recorded—history.

▲ The lens of a security camera shows all to the people looking at the screen behind the wall. In the modern world, a thin line separates the public's right to privacy and from the government's need to obtain information for security purposes.

TIMELINE

5th century B.C.	Chinese philosopher Mo-tzu produces the first written description of the principles of the camera obscura.
1727	Heinrich Schulze proves that silver compounds react to light.
1816	Joseph Niepce produces the first permanent negative image using a camera obscura.
1822	Louis Daguerre opens his first diorama, a forerunner of modern motion pictures.
1826	Niepce produces the world's first photograph.
1834	The Zoetrope is invented.
1839	Daguerre announces the invention of the daguerreotype. William Henry Fox Talbot announces the invention of the calotype.
1851	Frederick Scott Archer invents the wet-plate or collodion process.
1871	Dry-plate photography is invented by Richard Leach Maddox.
1876	Emile Reynaud presents animated comic stories using his Praxinoscope.
1880	George Eastman founds the Eastman Dry Plate Company.
1884	Eastman invents roll film.
1888	The first Kodak camera is sold.
1889	The Edison Manufacturing Company announces the invention of the Kinetograph movie camera.
1894	The first Kinetoscope opens in New York City.
1895	The Lumière brothers invent the Cinématographe.
1905	The world's first nickelodeon (movie theater) opens in Pittsburgh, PA.
1916	Western Electric introduces the Vitaphone sound film system.
1925	The Leica camera is introduced as the first 35-millimeter (35mm) camera.
1926	The first movie with sound is shown.
1930	Color film is invented.
1936	The first single-lens reflex (SLR) camera comes on the market.
1947	Edward Land introduces the Polaroid Land camera.
1990	Digital cameras are introduced.
1998	Megapixel (higher resolution) digital cameras for the consumer market are introduced.
2002	The first SLR digital camera that captures the same angle of view as a 35mm camera is launched.

GLOSSARY

ambrotype: a type of photograph that was mounted on a black background to resemble a daguerreotype, but which was much cheaper to produce

calotype: the earliest type of photograph that could be duplicated using negatives

camera obscura: literally, "dark room"; the name of a device of any size which was used to reflect an image through a small hole and project it onto a flat surface

collodion: a sticky liquid mixture used in wet-plate photography

daguerreotype: the first widely produced type of photograph

dry-plate photography: the gelatin-based photographic process invented by Richard Leach Maddox that made it possible to take action shots

emulsion: a sticky solution used to coat photographic plates or negatives

fix: to stop a photograph from darkening; to make it permanent

magic lantern: an early device that projected images on a screen

negative image: an image in which the light and dark areas are reversed when compared to the original subject

patent: a legal document that prevents people from stealing or making money from another person's idea or invention

photogenic drawing: a negative image produced by William Henry Fox Talbot's calotype process

plate: a flat piece of metal or glass used by early photographers instead of film

positive image: an image in which the light and dark areas match those of the original subject

tintype: a photograph developed on a thin metal plate that was painted black

wet-plate photography: the photographic process invented by Frederick Archer that used glass plates coated with collodion; also known as the collodion process

FOR MORE INFORMATION

Books

Bidner, Jenni. *The Kids' Guide to Digital Photography: How to Shoot, Save, Play With and Print Your Digital Photos.* New York: Lark, 2004.

Johnson, Neil L. *Photography Guide for Kids.* Washington, DC: National Geographic, 2001.

Pflueger, Lynda. *George Eastman: Bringing Photography to the People.* Berkeley Heights, NJ: Enslow Publishers, 2002.

Sproule, Anna. *Thomas A. Edison: The World's Greatest Inventor.* Woodbridge, CT: Blackbirch Press, 2000.

Wallace, Joseph. *The Camera.* New York: Atheneum Books for Young Readers, 2000.

Videos and DVDs

The Adventure of Photography. West Long Branch, NJ: Kultur International Films, 2003.

Alfred Stieglitz—The Eloquent Eye. New York: Winstar Home Entertainment, 2001.

Ansel Adams: A Documentary Film. Burbank, CA: Warner Home Video, 2003.

National Geographic's The Photographers. Washington, DC: National Geographic, 2003.

Web Sites

americanhistory.si.edu/cinema/index.htm An overview of the evolution of motion pictures, produced by the Photographic History Collection of the Smithsonian Institution.

memory.loc.gov/ammem/edhtm/edmvhm.html A Web site of the Library of Congress.

www.brightbytes.com/cosite/cohome.html This Web site explores the importance of the camera obscura and celebrates the history of photography.

www.howstuffworks.com/camera.htm/printable Viewers of this Web site will learn about all the parts of the camera and how they function.

www.npg.si.edu/exh/brady Viewers of this Web page will read about the life and work of Mathew Brady and view his extensive body of work online.

www.pbs.org/wgbh/amex/eastman/index.html Interactive features accompany information on PBS's film about George Eastman, founder of Kodak.

www.photographymuseum.com This virtual photography museum is dedicated to educating and showing photographs from around the world.

INDEX

Author Biography

A former elementary school teacher and educational software designer, Sandra Pobst enjoyed exploring new topics of study with students. Currently a freelance author, Sandra approaches each new project with the same curiosity and interest. She has written thirteen books for children and adults. Sandra has a B. S. in Elementary Education from Kansas State University. She resides in Austin, Texas.